Approachability:

The Key to Influence

How to be Approachable:

1. When someone new is entering your atmosphere

2. When someone you don't like or respect walks in.

3. When you are in a conflict setting.

Laura Hollands-Steck
Jean Hollands
Growth & Leadership Center

Introduction:

Why did we write this book?

- *We have worked with executives who were brilliant and diligent-- and lost their jobs.*

- *We have worked with managers who simply could not teach approachability to their favored subordinate or peer--their most unpopular team player.*

- *We have worked with executives who could not understand emotional intelligence.*

- *We have worked with the heartbreaking disappointment for those who hear: "and nobody wants to work for you."*

- *We have struggled with the executives from the C suite of Silicon Valley—those who just don't get "it."*

This book is about and for people who:

- *Know what approachability looks like, but can't explain it to others.*

- *Or for folks who don't seem to realize that others fear them.*

- *Or for folks who get frustrated when others don't understand their point immediately.*

- *Or for those who over-argue instead of trying to create a workable argument.*

- *Or for the person who over-stresses instead of over-compensating for differences.*

- *Or for those who just don't know how others perceive them.*

- *Or for those who lose credibility with a negative approach style.*

- *Or for you because you just want to figure out how to talk to your difficult and unapproachable person.*

Acknowledgements:

We offer our thank you to our loving husbands, Tom Rohrer and Ron Steck, our trusted advisors and content contributors. Ron, actually, is also a corporate coach and has been an insightful consultant and editor for this book.

A very special thanks to a major collaborator, Chris Michalski, who took the time to identify actual experiences of his own unapproachability in his career. With his coaching with GLC, and his own perseverance, he became a truly successful and approachable senior officer and Technical Fellow in High Tech Silicon Valley. His vulnerable contributions appear as comments from "Mr. Unapproachble."

We are also grateful to our own CEO of Growth & Leadership, Kent Kaufman who leads the way in being approachable in all of his interactions. Lastly, we appreciate all of our clients approachable and not, who make this work so satisfying and with whom we have been collaborating over the last 25 years.

Table of Contents

Forward

- Maybe you think you are already approachable.
- Maybe you don't care if you are or not.
- Maybe you know someone who needs this skill.
- Maybe you know someone who is losing everything because he or she has not had this book to read.

This short book is about communicating and influencing others with a positive approach. It's about an approach, behaviors, and skills you can use in difficult situations, to build new relationships, or even to negotiate tough agreements. In our work as executive coaches with the top leaders in Silicon Valley, we see that approachability gives people an extra edge by setting the stage for satisfying and productive working relationships.

Approachability is magic for careers—and *not* being approachable can be disastrous, on and off the job. Many of the people we coach are limited in their belief that getting the job done and getting results are *all* that matter. In doing this, they fail to see that the job gets done *through* others, not *despite* them. To get anything done that involves collaborating with other organizations, blending agendas, and balancing resources, demands attention to relationships!

A less interactional or reserved style is often seen as "cold" or "closed" and discourages people from interacting, sharing information, being persuaded, and being allied with someone and their mission. In contrast, being responsive around others, letting them in, and having a belief that people and relationships are *how* things get done, opens the door to results, synergy, greater influence, and even being seen as someone whom people like working for and with. And if you haven't noticed, those are the people who are easiest to promote.

We will talk about tricks, about do's and don'ts, and about why and how to become more approachable. We ask that you consider what's possible for you if you became more approachable—more folks with whom to consult, more easy negotiations and a more calm environment. Our hope is that you will see the impact, consequences, and benefits of this critical tool used in both business and personal interactions.

About the Authors:

Laura Hollands-Steck is President and Executive Coach of Growth & Leadership Center, a 25 year old corporate psychology organization. With an MA in Psychology, Steck quickly transferred key communication and conflict resolution skills with merging managers, teams and senior officers in High Tech companies. She has co-authored a book for Women's Leadership called *Same Game/Different Rules* and is frequently called on to coach leaders to be approachable in major corporate decisions and transitions.

Laura is also a national speaker and has a passion for empowering leaders and her theme is the same: be available, be open, and be authentic.

Jean Hollands is a national figure and founder and Chair of Growth & Leadership Center in California-- the first executive coaching company in Silicon Valley. She was featured in *New York Times, Harvard Business Review, Business Week* to *People Magazine* about her four previous executive coaching business books, **Silicon Syndrome, Optimistic Organizations, Red Ink Behaviors, Same Game, Different Rules.** Hollands is a national presenter who is known best for her surprising wit and grit at the podium.

With multiple appearances *on National News Programs, Oprah, Good Morning America, The Today Show and the Candice Bergen Show*, Hollands has learned best practices from the worst and the best officers from the C Suites in America.

Chapter One:

What is Approachability?

John Stanford was an executive and in a hurry. He didn't have time to be magnetic or charming. He didn't see the point in being more charismatic or even smiling when he met others. He saw it as a waste of effort, and, honestly, it was uncomfortable for him. When John, with his usual demeanor, *demanded* a good seat on the plane, he was informed there was nothing available.

As he made his way to the back of the plane and squeezed into his middle seat, it never occurred to him that his way of dealing with the ticket agent had anything to do with where he ended up on the plane. The ***man right after*** him in line, Harold Johnson, asked about getting an aisle seat near the front of the plane, and got it.

Here's why: ticket agent and supervisor, Mary Sampson, had been having a hard day. She just wanted to get home to her sick son. Yet one more cranky man, John Stanford, had just snapped at her and demanded a seat upgrade.

 Harold Johnson then took his place at the ticket counter, and noted that Mary was checking her watch and was probably waiting to get off duty. "This must be hard work, especially when you have people be so rude to you like that." Harold Johnson's words were so simple. Through his subtle investment in Mary, he stood out because he saw *her*, offered some empathy and wasn't seeing her as some obstacle to his objective. It wasn't hard to search a little harder and find him the aisle seat in row three.

Every day we encounter people like this who do not consider their impact on the people they interact with. And every day we encounter other people who interact with us in ways that help us to feel valued, important, and worth taking the time to treat well. The difference is real and tangible, and requires no thought to discern.

So what is Approachability?

1. **The experience others have when interacting with us.**
   When someone is approachable, the experience others have involves feeling welcomed, invited, respected, liked, and open.

   They feel better about themselves in the process of interacting with an approachable person. How often have you considered how others feel about themselves after having interacted with you?

2. **The skills and behaviors we use in interacting with others.**
   Approachability is also a set of keen emotionally intelligent skills and behaviors that result in creating that experience.

This includes, though is not limited to:

- *Open Body Language*
- *Responsiveness and Reaching Out*
- *Warmth and Humility*
- *Civility and Politeness*
- *Self-Awareness and Reading Others*
- *Willingness and Flexibility*
- *Listening and Curiosity*
- *Genuineness*
- *Interest and Inquiry*
- *Managing Conflict and Mending Fences*

People who have developed these skills typically have greater influence and traction for their causes. They get more disclosure, cooperation, and commitment they can count on. They seem to get agreement more often and people seem to want to give them what they want.

3. **The mindset, values and beliefs that underlie our behaviors.**
Approachability, and the behaviors associated with it are not an accident. They develop naturally out of a mindset that sees people as important and worth taking time for. They arise out of valuing of relationships, and believing that they are an essential pathway to producing business results.

If you see, value, and believe that attending to relationships is important, you treat them that *way* and pay attention to the impact you have. This involves a willingness to be other-oriented, to adopt another frame of reference that allows insight into the goals, needs, agendas, and experience of others.

Three Kinds of Unapproachables

The *Private Unapproachable* is the reserved type who has difficulty sharing anything personal or being empathetic. This person may have integrity and be quite competent but may not always consider the relationship aspects of the job at hand.

They will often not be friendly enough in stressful situations, and instead come across as cold and unconcerned about others. Because of this they often fail to sustain a loyal and faithful collegial support system.

Some executive do know that they may seem unfriendly. But, they make the mistake of thinking that because they are never aggressive, argumentative, or obnoxious, that others will see them as friendly. They believe that neutral is experienced as warm. They simply don't know that colleagues often need much more from them to feel at ease, and without it they will continue to see the unapproachables as cold and aloof.

> *Mr. Unapproachable says: "Sometimes I am just disconnected because I choose to be. It's been too much work to go through the effort. I put my best efforts into getting the job done, but I forget sometimes that I have to get the people done too."*

The *Public Unapproachable* is very open or welcoming in public settings. They can be serious, humorous, and even attentive, but inevitably the conversation road hits a dead-end because they fail to reveal enough to form the basis for a real conversation, connection, or rapport.

Despite the initial sense of approachability they generate, they and people attempting to talk with them find themselves feeling awkward and squirming for reasons to end the failed conversation. It doesn't take long for others to learn that when interacting with this person, it's best to settle for the superficial and move on quickly.

The *Tough Unapproachable* drives people away through some combination of aggressiveness, over-confidence, challenging, or harsh treatment of others. Often they are not aware of the kind of impact they have on others. From their perspective, they are looking for strong people to debate, or simply don't want to adapt their natural style to others because it's too much work.

These people often have big reputations, and the more timid folks shy away from interacting with them because they expect to get challenged and debated, rather than worked with and listened to.

After a while, these toughies may get curt, superficial responses from others who have felt "bruised" from past interactions. While conflict may not bother this type much, they underestimate the impact the conflict has on others, and the reputation they develop as someone to avoid. Even watching a tough approachable is hard on the more sensitive colleague.

Mr. Unapproachable learned that commenting negatively didn't work well. He stated: "I guess I have to stop being known as Dr. Doom—just because I usually know what is wrong with a process or project and I may say it too soon or too loudly—with usually too much back-up material."

He learned:
- *Approachability is looking like you want to talk to the other person and hear what they have to say.*
- *Approachability includes smiling.*
- *Approachability involves using a positive style of asking questions or making comments.*
- *Approachability is about noticing the feelings and reactions of others and yourself.*
- *Approachability is just staying open with people.*

There are many ways for someone to become unapproachable, but they all result in the same outcome: people avoiding or limiting interaction. Approachability is about listening to other people's perceptions about you, not just your good intentions. It's about caring and concern for others

As human beings, we are always sending out signals and messages to others about what we think and feel. We are either signaling some level of "come closer" or "move away."

Chapter Two:

The Approachability Test

Circle if a "yes" for each true statement:

1. I am uncomfortable in a social setting or in a no-host event, especially if I don't have a role or a position to play.

2. I forget to be cordial when I am highly focused on something.

3. If I don't approve of someone, it is hard for me to be open.

4. When I am in a conflict with someone, it is too difficult to be friendly or respectful at the same time.

5. On a team project, I usually choose an independent role.

6. If I am busy, I am openly irritated with people for distracting or interrupting me.

7. When someone new comes up to me, I am usually a bit wary or standoffish.

8. If I don't respect someone, I can't give that person the benefit of the doubt.

9. I don't often smile or warmly greet people in the halls.

10. When someone offers a view or suggestion on an issue, I usually debate or counter them, rather than offer understanding or validation.

11. In general, I don't concern myself with people's reactions to what I say or do.

12. I don't accept excuses, and I don't mind displaying my disapproval.

Scoring:

If you scored 1-2 yes answers, you are probably approachable.

If you scored 4-5 yes answers, you could improve your impact on others.

If you score 6 or more yes answers, becoming more approachable could transform your career. Read on.

In trying to assess your own approachability, here are some questions to ask yourself:

− In what situations do I care about how I come across to others?
− What is the down-side of not being approachable to my direct reports? My manager? My peers?
− When I think about others that I struggle with, do I consider what they really need from me?

- What good things could happen by paying attention to others' needs?
- What could I do to be more open without giving up on my principles?

Six-Second Approachability Test

In our company, we can simply ask our receptionist or business manager to tell us who is approachable. This person has the skills to feel warmth and likeability easily.

They can usually spot it in the first six seconds— when someone is entering our office asking for coffee or approaching one of our staff members.

Approachability is about listening to other people's perceptions about you, not just your good intentions about how you *hoped* to come across.

Getting the feedback can be a challenge. It involves finding enough people who would be open to providing the feedback, who also have enough emotional intelligence to spot problems, and who have an interest in your development and success.

These folks must also have the courage to give you feedback. This process means conveying to your proposed feedback people that you have a genuine interest in knowing more about how you come across to them.

Why Some People May Resist This Whole Idea

Most people are not able to evaluate their own communication skills. Rarely do they receive negative feedback, so they operate in their own "bubble," because they have no information to "pop" it. The unapproachable will not invite feedback about himself and does not usually seem interested in his interpretations anyway. Some people are simply not open to the ideas, perspective, and suggestions of others and are content to rely on their own perception and rules for interacting.

Some folks see the notion of being concerned for others as being unnecessary catering to others for the sake of being politically correct. Maybe they already have a very good position, the authority and power they want and just aren't concerned about how they are perceived by others.

In our over 25 years of coaching managers and executives, we have seen many executives who start out thinking this way. What they soon discover is that whether they were aware or not, they were in relationships, having significant (often negative) impacts, and were simply not being conscious of the unproductive environment they were creating.

> *Mr. Unapproachable: "I keep forgetting that perceptions are the truth. The perception about me is that I am cold, disinterested and indifferent. I wish they knew I did care. A lot of the time... I keep forgetting that feelings are fact. I have to listen for feelings, even though I am not used to doing that."*

When people get that they can take charge of the kind of impact they have on others, they almost always get actively engaged. They also find that generating productive working relationships is easier than they imagined, and often satisfying on a personal and professional level. We encourage folks like Mr. Unapproachable to be more curious about the people around them, to build trust by the way they communicate, and to be genuine, not manipulative, in their approach to others.

Chapter Three:

How to Become More Approachable

> *Mr. Unapproachable says: "If people ignore me or actively block me, I shouldn't expect others to not ignore me when I ignore them. I do care about the end customer, but I have to start showing I care about process along the way too."*

The Approachability Starter Kit

Here's a list of things to do become more approachable, in the moment and beyond.

1. Get feedback from managers, peers, and subordinates, through asking for it directly or from a 360 survey.
2. Set up feedback loops.
3. Take some interest in others most of the time, even if you are distracted or busy.
4. Acknowledge the points of others at least as much as we try to make our own points.
5. Make friendly gestures—smile, shake hands, look interested.
6. Let others go first if they want to, and don't answer with "yes, but."
7. Maintain a relaxed body posture, laugh, and ask about something outside of the current agenda.
8. Watch for signs of stress or frustration and invite them to talk about it.

9. Allow room for others to express their point of view, unhindered, and reflect back so they know we understand their point of view.
10. Use different greetings or start meetings with up- beat, appropriate humor.
11. Nod and try to match the energy of others.
12. Practice sounding approving.
13. Don't criticize just because you feel justified.
14. If there's some bad history between the two of you, start with a respectful line right away: "I know we both want to get the best results here."
15. Set out positive goals. "I'm hoping we can work through the decisions and we can collaborate. I know we often come from different view points."
16. Don't get distracted when meeting with someone new. Give them your full attention for at least a minute or two!
17. Look the other person in the eye—it may be uncomfortable. Do it anyway.
18. Consider the other person—Try to imagine how he or she feels meeting you.
19. Remember we could seem intimidating: it could be our position, our size, our voice, or our knowledge
20. Show mercy by giving the other person a chance, again.
21. Remember, influence is all we've really got.
22. Check out expectations often: "Is this what you were wanting?"
23. Don't forget to celebrate when you have made a connection.

About Body Language

People are always cueing each other with non-verbal signals. These signals, whether tone or body language, communicate whether we want someone to COME CLOSER or to MOVE AWAY.

Knowing and being conscious of our own signals is important, and so is learning to read the signals of others. When we see someone is on guard, we can calibrate how we approach them in a way that feels more comfortable. If a flamboyant extrovert tries to befriend the painfully shy introvert without calibrating his approach, he may cause a quick withdrawal

About Talking to Others:
A Message from Jean

"But I Hate Small Talk." Actually, most people really don't like small talk! We all like BIG talk, especially if it is about us, or our projects, or our reasons or opinions.

Networking meetings, luncheons with colleagues or business dinners are often intimidating, but there are networking techniques that make conversation with people you don't really know, or maybe even like, easier.

Our first technique is to learn that there are easy choices when talking to others to build rapport. We can either ask questions as a way to be interested in the other person or we can share and reveal our own ideas or interests as a way to be interesting. By inquiring about people, you are building rapport because people love to have others interested in them. Your curiosity helps people to feel important. Here are some examples of questions you can ask to get started:

- *Well, how do you like this offsite?*
  A more complex question can be--
- *How do you spend your days when you are not here?*
- *What keeps you up at night about this business?*
- *How is the team treating you?*
- *How is this role/event going for you?*
- *Tell me about your latest projects, expectations, opinion, family, interests, management...*

The second technique involves sharing and disclosing your own point of view, feelings, thoughts and ideas. When you feel comfortable enough to reveal your own thoughts or ideas, often others seem to relax.

Follow your own sharing with an inquiry, or invitation, for them to share their reaction to what you said. This can create the back-and-forth and the dialogue necessary for a real conversation.

When you are not good at small talk, and you must do it anyway, you can start with some level of humility or vulnerability:

- *These meetings are always hard for me.*
- *I am not good at some of these social moments.*
- *I am always uncomfortable starting conversations.*
- *I want to get to know new people but I'm a little slow at it.*
- *I never start conversations easily.*

Approachability and Influence:
A Message from Laura

We have observed that many executives and managers have an edge in their style that prevents them from being vulnerable in any way. The net effect is that others have a very difficult time feeling connected to them. Being able to connect to others through information, intellect, common goals, values, or perspectives, is the cornerstone of productive relationships. Without a relationship, the ability to influence others is severely affected. We often tell clients that their ability to influence others is in direct proportion to the quality of their relationships with other whom you may want to influence.

Why is influence important? Because we eventually do need and want things from people. The path to achieving results depends on our ability to persuade others who may have competing agendas with their attention and time devoted away from your causes.

25

We want our peers, bosses. teams and CEO to listen to our ideas and take action on our behalf. In order to influence someone to do something they are initially opposed to takes patience, great listening and a cultivation of that key relationship. It's not hard to imagine what happens to your ability to influence when you seem tense, speak with impatience, or use your frustration like a club.

In this way it is easy to see that the ability to influence is greatly affected by how people behave in stressful situations or in conflicts. Harsh behavior (or grace under pressure) will live on in people's experience of you, and can influence their willingness to be guided, lead, and persuaded in future interactions. The awareness and skill associated with shifting from a defensive, protective stance to an open, learning stance can make the difference between an average leader and an outstanding one.

Public figures and political officials offer great examples of how the principles of approachability work. In Hilary Clinton's campaign for president, she was dogged by criticisms that she lacked warmth. For some, she seemed to miss the vulnerability that allowed others to relate to her. Amazingly, however, her campaign received a huge boost when she showed emotion regarding how passionately she cared about what she was doing.

The perceptions may have been unfair, though they were very real to the people who had them. It wasn't until they had a sense of her vulnerability that they were able to connect more fully to her. Al Gore was perceived as sounding too "wooden" and John McCain has struggled with the perception that he was angry.

These and other candidates try to take actions to portray themselves as real people, with real lives and concerns, as a way to overcome negative perceptions and allow the voters to feel a sense of connection. Without the connection there is very little influence.

If you want to improve your influence, consider these questions:

- *What is your reputation as a communicator?*
- *Are you different as a public presenter?*
- *Does your personal warmth come through?*
- *In what situations are you more approachable than others and why?*

Remote Communication: Email, Phone and Web

Remote communication lacks most of the cues that allow us to "read" one another accurately. Brief messages with the "Hello" can seem curt, impatient and angry. It's easy to misunderstand and be misunderstood.

What's worse is any mistakes can live on forever, not only in people's minds, but in email messages that get forwarded on to more and more people. Because of their limitations, phone calls and emails can kill a deal, a relationship, or a partnership.

It's wise to be extremely vigilant about how and what we communicate in an email to anyone. Always re-read before sending. Don't send if angry—wait until the upset recedes, and carefully communicate what needs to be said, keeping in mind the need to maintain the relationship beyond the upset. Try being a bit paranoid about how things could be taken and rephrase to eliminate the risks, and convey regard and consideration.

Chapter Four:

What Happens If Someone Is Not Approachable?

Negative impressions can come back to bite people if they haven't focused on their approachability. Typically, early on in relationships people are trying to assess who's an ally, who's friendly, who can be trusted. If they can't get approval easily, feel uncomfortable, or insecure, they can come to quick conclusions that aren't easily overcome.

If the initial conclusions are reinforced over time, if the people continue to feel unimportant, dismissed, and disliked, the relationship can become adversarial. In other words, people may be more inclined to treat you in ways they feel you have treated them by being unresponsive, sabotaging, critical, and withholding.

> *Mr. Unapproachable: "I wish someone would have given me feedback or told me about these skills earlier, before I impacted my career so negatively. I know NOW that it is my responsibility to ask for feedback…and listen well!*

The Consequences of Not Being Approachable

Here are the most common negative consequences described to us by the many people we have coached:

- Didn't get hired for the job
- Passed over for recognition
- Not nominated
- Delayed or lost promotion
- Demoted or diminished authority
- Not included as member of influential committee
- Diminished awards, bonuses, and raises
- People avoiding working for/with the person
- Refused when asked for key favors or allowances
- Loss of strategic allies and backing
- People refusing to be influenced
- Lost direct reports because of poor relationship
- Terminated for inability to work on or with a team

By the way, even if you are an individual contributor, you will still have to overlap with peers and other managers or customers at times. People will observe you!

The Excuses

> *Mr. Unapproachable says: "People can't always see my good intentions. They have to feel them. Well, some people do anyway. I have to recognize those colleagues who need me to be particularly approachable..."*

"I'm too busy to be open"

We know work and life is happening at warp speed and it's easy to be too busy and preoccupied. We know people prefer to stay focused. It doesn't really take as much time as people think to show concern, offer suggestions, or lend a hand for a few minutes. That time, concern and effort is essentially an investment in the relationship, and refusing to provide it is a withdrawal. We also know people want to be successful, selected, promoted, included or seen as influential.

Simple things can suffice when time is limited:

- **Make eye contact**
- **Smile**
- **Offer a welcoming, "Hello. How is your day going?"**
- **Briefly explaining the lack of time or availability**
- **Offer times to connect**

"I don't want to sound like a phony manipulator!"

When our clients suggest the above, we answer with, "Don't worry; you couldn't be one if you tried! Because of their acquired strengths and where they fall on the spectrum of approachability, it's not likely that they could come off as too friendly, inauthentic or a phony. Incidentally, babies are usually all born with approachability. The technique is rubbed out of us by difficult experiences, rewards for being cool or modeling by others that an icy approach works.

The key is to cultivate an authentic interest and value for the colleagues with whom you work. It's not about being a salesman, or about manipulating people.

The truth is that being complimentary or warm towards others can feel uncomfortable, vulnerable, and risky in the beginning. Remember that others experience these things as welcoming and affirming, and will likely reinforce you positively for doing them. If it's uncomfortable, it means you are probably doing it right.

"I'm not a pleaser or an accommodator by nature."

It's not necessary to be an accommodator to be more approachable. Being more attentive interested, and inquiring doesn't require a complete change of personality. Being more curious and positively inquiring doesn't change the person, but alters the impact they have on others. It's simply a conscious choice, one that has significant impact on the quality of relationships and the benefits to go with it.

...

We, at GLC, had a grumpy Chief Technology Officer at one point that was known as "mean spirited and quite a tyrant." His President and HR person said that nobody wanted to be around him, that people were transferring and leaving the company because of what it was like to work for and with him.

He was very difficult to engage, though after his third session with us, we were finally able to get him to agree to try one thing. Smile once an hour for a month. He was sure he couldn't pull it off!

Three weeks later, the company President called to say that our man was a changed guy. Everyone was commenting on how relaxed and easy-going he had become. The President thanked us for the good work we had done with him. Sometimes a little goes a long way.

Our client reported: "I didn't do anything. Well, I did that smile once an hour. Wow! Did I get feedback about how relaxed and friendly I seemed!"

Chapter Five:

Approachability: Grace and Skill in Difficult Moments

How we behave in difficult moments registers deeply with others, reassures them that we treat people well, that we can be approached about difficult subjects in the future, and it potentially builds emotional capital in our relationships.

> *Mr. Unapproachable says: "If I don't approve of someone, it's hard for me to be open, and I don't give approval easily. Guess I am pretty judgmental. For so long when I was in conflict, I didn't get how to be collaborative."*

Grace is about taking the high road, maintaining a sense of the big picture when we interact in the moment, and a commitment to bring our best to a difficult situation. It is extremely important to take the high road. Our intention to seek the best outcome and treat people well influences the outcome of conflicts before we even open our mouths. If we can stay less reactive, we minimize triggering the worst in others.

Skill is about models and using what you know *when* it's needed. Anytime there is a disagreement that escalates—we need to pull out and use what we know about conflict resolution.

To start with, it helps to think that successful conflict skills involve juggling two balls: one ball is our needs, reasons, and perspective, and the other ball are the needs, reasons, and perspective of the person we are dealing with. It's important to carefully identify the content of both balls and consider what we missed in giving to the other person.

How to Approach the Unapproachable: Meeting for the First Time

We know the person we are about to meet is not friendly. We've heard he doesn't smile, interrogates rather than inquires, and seems to take no interest in people on a personal level. He can be critical of new ideas and closed to others input. We are pretty sure he is not excited about meeting us.

> *More from Mr. Unapproachable: "I don't have trouble with the technical people who speak my language. But I experienced first hand the cause and effect of not giving enough approval to folks. I experienced peers leaving me out of the loop after certain interactions...*

Grace and skill—act respectful; be open to learning about what's important to the other person. Practice patience. **Remember not to take his demeanor personally**. Even if we don't receive the response we want, it's still our job to be approachable and let him learn to relax around us. As time goes by, we will have a chance to form a positive working relationship, but at first, it may have to be in his form.

Remember that everyone has the following five Universal Primal Needs—(even when they cannot express them.). We want:

1. **To be understood,**
2. **To be accepted**
3. **To be trusted**
4. **To be recognized**
5. **To be in control**

Approachability in a Conflict

> *Mr. UA says, "I don't respond well to attack. Sometimes it may not even be an attack, but if my judgment or my answers are not taken well, I guess I take it personally. Sometimes it's just a misunderstanding. I need to react slower and to listen first.*

Step One:

Reframe the issue benignly.
Most of us want to be understood in spite of an irrational presentation. Find a way to try to understand the other's needs even when he or she seems to be accelerating a problem.

Step Two:

Use Reflective Listening.
We believe that 80% of conflicts would dissolve instantly if people dedicated time to listening, without agenda, to each other. Active Listening or

Reflective Listening is when we *willingly* reflect in our own words what we hear from the other person regarding content, issues, concerns, affect, values, and needs.

"I'm hearing that you feel it's really important to the project and your team... Am I on the right track about this?"

Step Three:

Own your own contributions to the situation or conflict.
It seems so rare that people actually acknowledge their own faults and mistakes that when it happens, it's like finding a gold nugget in a pan full of sand. It can quickly take the fight out of a situation, and makes it easy for others to relax, open up, and collaborate rather than compete.

Try: *"I know I didn't communicate with you and your team about the changes we had made, and I know it has caused a lot of headaches for you."*

Step Four:

The Six Magic Words in Conflict: "I'm sorry this happened to us."
Apologies, compassion and empathy all contribute to a softening of position, of attitudes, and defensiveness. If we are not attacking, people don't need to defend and we are able to have a different kind of conversation.

Step Five:

Bring your intent to learn to the conflict, not your intent to protect.
If we are not trying to protect ourselves, we can listen, learn, be curious, and get educated about new information. Our openness influences the interaction, and makes it more likely that others will be open to our views as well.

Mr. Unapproachable says, "When I'm angry, it is hard to shift. Sometimes I even have a good reason to be mad. But it is a total waste of effort and a drain on me, so I want to move on. I've had to learn to view other people's actions without assigning a negative motive. This is not easy.

Approachability and Crisis Moments

The customer is furious. The boss is on the phone. Your head is pounding. Everything feels like it has to be done in the next five minutes, and there's no way.

In saunters Bob Bellingham—the guy who usually likes to chat about the latest office gossip, sports event, or his latest golf game—threatening to hijack your precious few minutes. Is this *really* a good time to be approachable?

Or maybe it's someone else's crisis that screams for our attention when we are waist deep in our own. Either way, we are stuck with the same dilemma—us or them.

If we ignore these people, we may miss information we will need at some point, we may undermine the chances of gaining a future mentor, champion or an ally in our next big project. Or maybe it will come back to bite us in the future when we need assistance, attention, or support in getting through our next crisis. Maybe one of these people will end up being the decision-maker on a key role, job, or resource that we want. It can be small world, and relationships often last a lot longer than the crisis-of-the-day.

So How Do We Become Approachable in a Crisis?

What would it take to muster up a decent greeting, a civil excuse, and ask the Bob Bellingham to visit another time? Or to stay open, lift our head from the task for a few moments, give the person our genuine regard, suggest we have only a few minutes, announce our own crisis and promise another meeting?

What it takes is a little time, a little thought, and valuing people and relationships by being decent in our actual transactions with them.

"John, I know you want to talk now. I wish we could. I am in the middle of a back-breaker for me. I can talk for two minutes now, though anything more than that and we'll probably need to find another day."

40

When the Boss, Co-Workers or the Company Has Killed Our Approachability:

Maybe we felt bruised, insulted, discounted, or on the bad end of someone's hurtful behavior that has seriously damaged their trustworthiness.

There will be times when our mindset is negative and we simply can't find a way to sound approving or reassuring to some people in the organization.

Or there are other times when the company culture has become so unpleasant and untenable that sounding positive and encouraging is more than difficult. It is not easy to be positive when morale is low.

When trust is an issue, it is hard to put on a cordial face and "make nice" because it feels insincere. But MOST OF THE TIME it's in our best interest to continue working with this person and look for opportunities to rebuild the relationship over time.

Why? Because enemies don't typically disappear, and can even spawn new enemies, factions, and coalitions that can work against us. We see so many executives destroy their ability to lead by neglecting to work through and repair relationships that hold the political keys to their success.

The bottom line about company politics is that the quality of our relationships determines our ability to influence and obtain the backing we can count on. It's naive to think we are ever *NOT* involved in these "political" relationships. The question is: are we managing them?

When morale or outlook about a person, division, or company is the issue, there is real risk of becoming the pessimistic black hole that sucks the life out of most interactions with people. This kind of unapproachability drives people far away, and with them goes the possibility that you will be seen as a resilient leader that others support and follow.

So what can we do? As we mentioned before, the first step is to beg, borrow or steal a perspective or attitude that allows us to maintain poise, realistic optimism, and the motivation to keep trying.

Good leaders frame things positively, to themselves and to others. Here are a few perspectives that many people find useful in difficult circumstances:

- **People (and companies) are doing the best they know how**
- **Learning and change take time**
- **Trust can be rebuilt**
- **People are pursuing understandable needs and intentions, even though they make mistakes**
- **Things can improve with sustained effort, focus, and support**

The mindset we bring to the interactions will affect the people we interact with even if we don't' say anything because our facial expressions, tone, and body language convey it. Your face tells all.

The second step is to take some action to start moving yourself, the other person or company in the right direction. Here are some example actions:

1. Get an appropriate sounding board to express yourself and see if you can move your negative thinking out of your way.
2. Get perspective and ideas from others who are feeling more resourceful than you.
3. Create a plan with a beginning, middle and end to rectify the situation.
4. Talk to your boss or co-worker, one more time about what they need from you and what you need from them to improve the situation.
5. Own any part of the situation you have yet to take responsibility for.
6. Increase your outside activities to diffuse over-focusing on negativity.
7. Go to the Human Resources Department for support.
8. Get a coaching program.
9. Take a vacation and re-charge.

Chapter Six:
Approachability and Broken Relationships

When the Other Guy is the Enemy—Or We Just Hate His Guts

We're sorry if you were looking for a way out. The same rules apply. The relationship still matters; one way or another, directly or indirectly. A broken relationship will come back to bite you in ways you won't even anticipate. We simply need to give ourselves the very best chance for things to improve at some point.

It's important to stay focused on the greater goal, be the bigger person, and use our best communication skills. With the big picture in mind it's easier to stay civil, polite, and patient, and give the other person more chances to get it *right* with us.

We don't advocate being a sycophant or a manipulator. Instead, bring your best, principled, and considerate self to the interaction, and over time, the relationship will improve.

When It Is Hard to Forgive

When we are unable to forgive, some of us simply withdraw. Some even sulk, holding on to our own personal bad history and interpretations of that history. Resentment is toxic. It kills initiative and creativity. It colors every subsequent event, and it ultimately limits options, possibilities, and progress. At some point we need to be responsible for the effect the lack of forgiveness has on us, the other person, and the environment we share.

Great leaders find ways to resolve conflicts and repair relationships.

> *From Mr. Unapproachable: "There has been enough conflict in my group that they barely use me. I can hardly bring myself to make eye contact, let alone smile. Yet, I know this is the beginning of the way out of my dilemma. What I have done has closed the doors. They exclude me in meetings. Of course, I used to just miss the meetings my boss called because I thought he didn't know anything. I have to start going to those meetings again and stop waiting to 'catch' him doing something wrong."*

Techniques for Approachability When Faced with Broken Relationships and Old Grudges:

1. Start slowly. Get the perspective of someone else who knows and likes the person we hold the grudge against. Ask them for suggestions.

2. Put on his shoes. Find a way to understand the behavior of the person so we feel less threatened, offended, and hurt.

3. Get clear on your part in the whole problem; feeling less like a victim can make it easier to forgive.

4. Examine ourselves and our patterns. Maybe it's not all about the other person: how often are we angry with others, mistrust them, or write them off? What's our level of tolerance for the mistakes of others? Is there a pattern over the last month, year, or ten years?

5. Try compassion: do we remember (if you can't, then imagine) when others were unwilling to forgive us, when they wrote us off, and stopped listening to us? Think about how doing this to others may not fit with the kind of person we want to be.

6. Be more conscious and intentional about our communications, verbal and non-verbal. Our words, tone, and body language affect everyone around us and set the stage for how they respond.

7. In the big picture, how much angst is this really worth?

8. Think of the positive impact on all the people who are affected by the broken relationship and the relief for individuals, teams, and even organizations would feel if the tension were gone.

9. Ask ourselves what needs to be developed in us to handle our intolerance of others?

10. Make any kind of apology that we sincerely can offer:

a. "I'm sorry we haven't been on the same page, have we?"
b. "I'm sorry my style has been hard on you."
c. "I'm sorry we've had to go through this."

11. Acknowledge that things have always been a bit difficult between the two of you.

12. Express our intention to repair or improve the relationship and invite their intention to do the same:
    a. "I want to stop the strain between us."
    b. "I want us to find a way to work better together going forward. How could we start?"
    c. "I know that was a challenging situation for both of us, and I want us to start again. Are you willing to give this another try?"

13. Always begin with owning your contributions to the problem:
    a. "I know I was impatient with you, and I seemed to be obsessed with getting the job done my way."
    b. "My demands were probably very hard on you given you had such a short deadline."
    c. "I wish I had been more cooperative and concerned about your point of view."

14. Give empathy if you can.

15. Go the extra mile and make regular attempts to clear the air.

16. Reward yourself for making efforts.

> **Mr. Unapproachable says: *"I didn't forgive management
> until I realized that I don't always see the big picture and it
> is my job to keep the communication working."***

Working with People We Don't Like

Of course it happens that we will have to work with
the person we don't like or respect. Suppose there's
a history of disagreements, no track record of mutual
respect, and yet the two of us are selected to lead a
project.

We need to keep the mindset of a leader facing
adversity and be the person who shows compassion
and understanding first. This is a good opportunity
to focus on getting the relationship done as a way to
get the job done by remembering to address the
relationship first and continuing with openness to the
other's views, needs, and agendas.

Start positively: *"Mary, I know we have to work
together on this project, and I really want to have
this go well for us. I regret that we have had some
rough interactions in the past, though I think we
can do great work together. How would you like to
start?"*

Set out a new positive Goal: *"I know you want to
be productive with this project too, so I'm hoping
we can create mutual criteria that address both our
visions for this project."*

When you have a Hard Problem to Solve

Yes, it all comes down to having a good attitude through tough situations. It means managing your reactions when things go wrong, and staying approachable so the problem can be worked through. It's learning how we affect people simply by our personal approach, especially if we are intimidating, stubborn, closed-minded, over-persuasive, or unreadable.

Don't show up to a tough negotiation loaded with resentments and old triggers. Prepare by identifying the top five things this person can do that upsets, frustrates, enrages, or makes you want to flee.

This process helps in writing the dreaded evaluation report that so many managers detest.

Then identify the unproductive or even destructive behaviors brought about by these triggers. Here is a sample list:

Top Five Triggers:

1. *Missing commitments*
2. *Getting dates wrong*
3. *Misrepresenting progress*
4. *Criticizing me in meetings*
5. *Implying I don't know enough*

Unproductive Behaviors

1. *Publicly criticizing the person for failing the schedule*
2. *Overtly exasperated and indignant expressions*
3. *Calling people liars*
4. *Getting defensive and counter-attacking*

We can use these lists to better manage ourselves in the upcoming meeting or negotiation. Make it a priority to *not* react to those triggers in the same way, and make it an agenda to stay above the provocation. Stay focused on the goals, and resist escalating the difficult situation.

How to Navigate the Mine Field

1. Identify our common ground and areas of alignment first.

2. Outline and honor the differences in approach and perspective.

3. Listen and reflect their content, feelings, goals, preferences, and beliefs

4. Acknowledge mistakes in your own communication as they occur—don't wait.

5. Be diligent about articulating expectations clearly and forming agreements about which both parties can be comfortable.

6. Build in feedback, asking for yours first and then asking permission to give the other person constructive feedback.

7. Maintain the perspective that we, *together*, can make this work.

The Possibilities of Relapse

We can begin to slide into the old and favored habits, slowly shutting our door more often, or answering phones with a quick, "Johnson here."

Take a quick look at the inventory of your moods, actions and attitudes. Go to your feedback loops that you created. Acknowledge your triggers. These triggers can make us intolerant and disagreeable. Often your response is unconscious.

Identify what have you felt negatively about and how you framed that situation in your head and out loud to others.

Even if we make progress, things can slip back without maintenance. When we slip:

- Ask for regular feedback on how things are going and how they could go better.
- Listen more attentively while we are on the phone, and take time to clarify our understanding.
- First listen to the other person's tone of voice.

- Manage our own tone of voice.
- Before sending emails, read them to make sure they are delicate, non-accusing, and give the benefit of the doubt.
- Reduce negative or critical language to avoid triggering the other person. Remember that people will see our verbal and written expressions as our "brand."
- Behave with integrity by making and keeping your commitments with this person
- Be extra responsive with this person and his team, noting the level of urgency and try to respond accordingly.
- Make overt gestures toward this person that show we understand what's important to them.
- Own your own mistakes, apologize quickly, and make amends for missteps and misdeeds immediately.

There Are Times When Being Approachable Is Inappropriate

We get to choose our approachable moments. There are, of course, times in life when it is much better to play hardball and choose to be not open or friendly.

It's okay to have some situations when you may withhold thoughts and friendly gestures—like in the courtroom, dealing with harassment, or during a legal negotiation. It is, however, important to think of these as exceptions, not the rule.

Chapter Seven:

Why Some Folks Just Don't Get It

Here are some of the reasons why some of our clients just couldn't get it at first:

- Their boss brought out the bulldog approach in them.

- They were afraid of being a show off, and isolated themselves too much.

- They never got this feedback from others; now they just don't believe it.

- They been betrayed by people they befriended and didn't recover.

- They got too attached to their judgment of others, and decided the "stupid" people were not worth their time.

- Mentors and role models did not model approachability, and they seemed successful anyway.

- They felt too shy to reach out to others.

- They felt humiliated when they tried to do small talk.

- They thought it was easier just to avoid rather than do the intensive interaction it would take to finish the task with someone else

- It was a lot of work to change.

- They didn't believe it was possible.

Chapter Eight:
Good News: Approachability Can Be Taught!

Yes, anybody can learn it. Today. Now. It takes practice. It takes real intention and a sustained commitment. It takes curiosity about why and how being unapproachable has come about. And it takes courage to hear how others see us in ways that affect our working relationships. The reward is influence.

You can teach approachability to other with positive reinforcement when they seem more accommodating or friendly. If, in fact, you get permission to help the other person to become more approachable, don't pounce or preach. Then keep checking to see that you are modeling the behaviors you want to teach.

Steps to Teaching Approachability:

1. Set goals.
2. Solicit feedback loops.
3. Receive feedback--staying open and non-defensive.
4. Do reflective listening.
5. Incorporate feedback in all avenues.
6. Experiment with new behavior.
7. Continue to solicit feedback.
8. Refine your new behavior
9. Turn behavior into habit

How to Teach Approachability

A great way to being teaching approachability is to simply model it through behavior, through every interaction, or negotiation. People who are unapproachable probably don't realize their style.

Having something to compare and contrast is sometimes a profound teacher. Feedback is essential, though often it requires some form of relationship for it to be accepted—concerned boss-to-employee, safe peer-to-peer, and trusted employee-to-boss. How the feedback is given can teach as well:

"I noticed something that happened in the last meeting I'd like to talk with you about if this is a good time. I have done similar things myself and didn't recognize it at the time, and wondered if you would be open to a little feedback from me?

...When you told Dave that he didn't know what he was talking about, the whole meeting seemed to shut down. Did you notice that? ...I know you weren't trying to have that effect, though when we say things too harshly, sometimes people stop wanting to interact with us, and that can create a lot of problems down the road."

Or:

"I know that you are a great contributor here, and I wanted to give you a small bit of feedback that might help you get across to others more effectively. Would you be interested in what I noticed in that last meeting?"

When a colleague sees us as his advocate and ally, you can say almost anything to him and he will take it in. So, in order to be an effective teacher, it's necessary to use approachability skills to form enough of an authentic relationship to exert influence

Coaching and active mentoring are the most effective means of teaching these skills. Many of the approaches we take in coaching executives apply to becoming more approachable. We use the following techniques:

- Concentrate on self-reflection issues, triggers, and intentions.
- Understand other person's behavior, needs, agendas, and perspective.
- Manage thinking and staying optimistic and resourceful.
- Experiment and find what works.
- Cultivate feedback sources and allies in the workplace.
- **The "me too" syndrome. Don't respond with, "Oh, that happens to me too." This diminishes the other person's experience.**
- **Watch for "yes, but" from the other person. It means you have not reflected his viewpoint adequately.**

Teaching someone to keep the focus on unapproachable behavior provides feedback in the moment. It helps decipher other peoples' reactions and needs which accelerates the learning process.

Chapter Nine:
Approachability Works

Being approachable is really not that difficult. It can take only a moment to decide to be different, and a few more moments to take action--getting the feedback, training, or coaching to assist you. Small changes in a mindset can yield big changes in behavior, just like small gestures can open doors to better interactions with others.

A boss may delegate you to be the unapproachable tough guy. This boss does not have the courage to share bad news or feedback himself. So you may join the trap of bringing bad news for a weak manager. This is when approachability could work for you.

Just this week one of our clients told us, "I have to understand that I've been reinforced for aggressive behavior throughout my whole career. But getting to that next behavior means working out those relationships I have neglected. It's not working for me anymore to run interference for my boss. It's tough but I need to change what I'm doing. I don't need to be the bad guy anymore. I need to look at my own career now."

Once Again, the Consequences of Not Being Approachable:

- Lost business
- Lost partnerships
- Lost promotions
- Lost results
- Lost compromises
- Lost relationships
- Lost champions and advocates
- Lost sales
- Lost influence and effectiveness
- Lost opportunities

> *Mr. Unapproachable: "I learned the hard way. I look back on how when I ignored my manager, he ignored me back. I got myself in a big hole with him. I had to stop worrying about others missing technical deadlines—that was really his job to manage. I had to change. It's interesting how differently I interpret him now. He's not an enemy, and I've learned I can interact with him and stop reacting...It is working!"*

Everyone has a chance to improve in this area. We hope that in reading these words that it will inspire people to make changes or to help others make a change.

We know people can change because we experience it every day, and the payback is incredible.
Let's remember, get the business done and add on that smile, a kind word, a thoughtful gesture or inviting question.

Being approachable is easy, fun, promotes influence and prevents a submerged pain that can last a career lifetime.

Stay approachable!